WHALES
IN AMERICAN HISTORY

NORMAN D. GRAUBART

PowerKiDS
press
New York

Published in 2015 by The Rosen Publishing Group, Inc.
29 East 21st Street, New York, NY 10010

First Edition

Editor: Amelie von Zumbusch
Photo Research: Katie Stryker
Book Design: Colleen Bialecki

Photo Credits: Cover Hulton Archive/Getty Images; p. 4 David Ashley/Shutterstock.com; p. 5 Photos.com/Thinkstock; p. 6 Brian J. Skerry/National Geographic/Getty Images; p. 7 Fuse/Thinkstock; p. 9 James R.D. Scott/Flickr/Getty Images; p. 10 Buyenlarge/Archive Photos/Getty Images; pp. 12, 20 Apic/Hulton Archive/Getty Images; p. 13 (bottom) Education Images/Universal Images Group/Getty Images; p. 13 (top) Earle Keatley/iStock/Thinkstock; p. 15 Photos.com/Thinkstock; p. 16 Currier and Ives/The Bridgeman Art Library/Getty Images; p. 17 Ken Lucas/Visuals Unlimited/Getty Images; p. 18 Science and Society Picture Library/Getty Images; p. 19 DEA Picture Library/De Agostini/Getty Images; p. 21 Achimdiver/Shutterstock.com; p. 22 Alexy Mhoyan/Thinkstock.

Library of Congress Cataloging-in-Publication Data

Graubart, Norman D., author.
 Whales in American history / by Norman D. Graubart. — First edition.
   pages cm. — (How animals shaped history)
 Includes index.
 ISBN 978-1-4777-6773-3 (library binding) — ISBN 978-1-4777-6774-0 (pbk.) — ISBN 978-1-4777-6630-9 (6-pack)
 1. Whaling—United States—History—Juvenile literature. 2. Whales—Juvenile literature. 3. Whales—Conservation—Juvenile literature. I. Title.
 SH383.2.G73 2015
 639.2'8—dc23
                                        2014001270

Manufactured in the United States of America

CPSIA Compliance Information: Batch #WS14PK5: For Further Information contact Rosen Publishing, New York, New York at 1-800-237-9932

Whales are Earth's largest animals. They live in all kinds of ocean **climates**. Many **species**, or types, of whales live in the waters off the United States. Americans have hunted whales for centuries. Long before Europeans arrived, Native American tribes on both the East and West Coasts hunted whales.

Humpback whales live in all of Earth's oceans. They are known for the long patterns of sounds they make to communicate. These noises are called whale songs.

Sperm whales, like the one in this nineteenth-century image, were dangerous to hunt because they often fought back. However, catching them could be very profitable.

In the middle of the nineteenth century, the United States became the center of the world's whaling **industry**. Whales are still important to us today. They are considered to be among the world's most intelligent animals. Aquariums around the world keep them in giant tanks so that scientists can study them.

Scientists divide whales into toothed whales and **baleen** whales. Instead of teeth, baleen whales have large, comblike structures called baleen. Baleen catches krill. These are the tiny, shrimplike animals that baleen whales eat. Humpback whales, gray whales, and right whales are all baleen whales. In the past, these species were all heavily hunted by American whalers, or whale hunters.

The right whale got its name because early whalers considered it the right whale to hunt. It swam slowly and floated after it was killed, making it easy to catch and bring back to shore.

Whales breathe air. When they surface to breathe through their blowholes, they let out a spray of air and water. In the past, whale hunters used this spray as a way to spot whales.

Toothed whales have teeth, just as humans do. They are hunters. They use their teeth to chew the food they catch. Dolphins are a kind of toothed whale. Orcas are as well. Orcas are also called killer whales. Sperm whales are toothed whales, too.

SPERM WHALES

Sperm whales are some of the largest whales in the ocean. Adults can be up to 60 feet (18 m) long. They weigh as much as 45 tons (41 t). They travel around Earth's oceans in groups, called pods.

In their heads, sperm whales have a waxy substance called **spermaceti**. Electric lights were not invented until the late nineteenth century. Before that, candles and oil lamps made from spermaceti were considered the best light sources.

Sperm whales sometimes make a substance called **ambergris** in their digestive systems. This used to be used to make perfume. Ambergris and spermaceti made sperm whales very valuable to whalers.

Sperm whales dive deep into the ocean to find food. Average dives last over half an hour and reach depths of 1,312 feet (400 m). However, deeper dives are not uncommon.

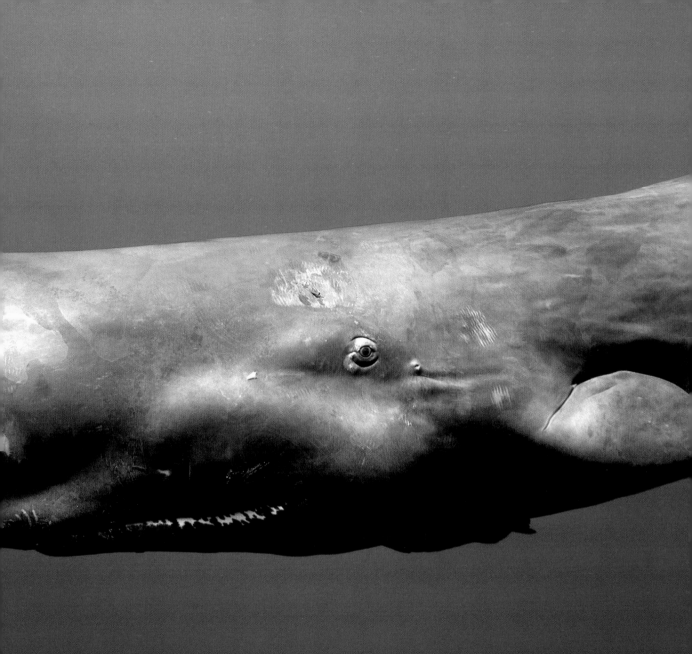

In the Pacific Northwest, Native American tribes hunted whales for many centuries. The Makah tribe, which still lives in northwestern Washington, hunted whales at least 2,000 years ago. Whale meat has traditionally been a key food for the Makah people. The Makahs also made furniture and tools from whalebones.

Native American peoples in New England hunted whales, too. These tribes mostly recovered dead or dying whales that washed up on or near the shore, called drift whales. Whaling was especially important to the Wampanoag Indians, who lived on Martha's Vineyard and Nantucket. These two islands are now part of Massachusetts.

The native peoples of Alaska also hunted whales. In this photo from the early twentieth century, a group of Inupiat hunters are launching a whale-hunting boat.

1712

Colonists and Native Americans begin to hunt sperm whales off the coast of Nantucket.

1861-1865

The Civil War badly hurts the whaling industry. The Confederate navy sinks many Northern ships.

1675　1700　1725　1750　1775　1800　1825

1851

Herman Melville publishes *Moby-Dick*, a book about the voyage of a whaling ship. It is now one of the most famous American novels.

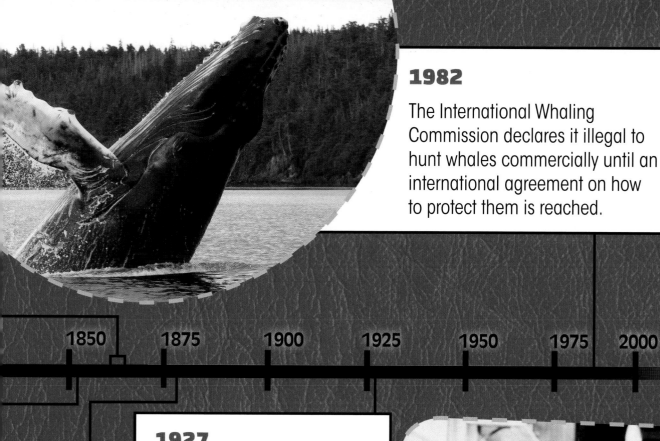

1982

The International Whaling Commission declares it illegal to hunt whales commercially until an international agreement on how to protect them is reached.

1850　　1875　　1900　　1925　　1950　　1975　　2000

1927

The *John R. Mantra*, of New Bedford, Massachusetts, makes the last American **commercial** whaling voyage.

1879

Thomas Edison invents the electric lightbulb, which will eventually replace oil lamps all over the world.

13

THE GOLDEN AGE

Early colonists caught whales close to shore, much as the Native Americans did. By the eighteenth century, whales became harder to find off the coast of New England. Therefore, New Englanders sailed far into the Atlantic Ocean to find whales. Beginning in the 1790s, they began sailing around South America's southern tip to hunt whales in the Pacific Ocean!

The American golden age of whaling began around 1815. Cities such as New Bedford, Massachusetts, became famous for whaling. In 1857, 10,000 men worked in the whaling industry in New Bedford. That's more people than lived in Los Angeles at the time!

This nineteenth-century print shows American whalers in the South Sea, which is another name for the South Pacific Ocean. Their journey to reach it was long and dangerous.

15

Unusually for their time, whaling ships often had **integrated** crews. African Americans, Native Americans, and European Americans worked together. However, life on whaling ships was rough. Crewmen hunted whales in small whaleboats. They cut the fat from the dead whales. Then they boiled it down in greasy try pots on the ship's deck.

> Whaleboats were light and narrow. Each one had a harpooner, who threw or fired a harpoon into the whale. It also had four oarsmen and one man to steer the boat.

Along with whalebone, whalers also made scrimshaw on sperm whale teeth. People who carve scrimshaw are called scrimshanders.

Crewmen earned money based on how many whales they caught. They often did not get very much money by the end of the long trip. Sometimes, whaling voyages would last longer than four years. Crewmen dealt with the boredom by carving detailed designs on whalebones. This art form was called **scrimshaw**.

THE USEFUL WHALE

Ambergris and spermaceti were important products to early whalers, but they were not the only ones. Electric power had not been discovered yet, and most people used oil-burning lamps to light their houses. Whale oil lit city streets, too. Whales have a lot of fat. Whaling crews heated the fat to turn it into the kind of oil that was used in lamps.

Baleen was often used to make umbrellas. The ribs over which the cloth was stretched were made from it. Umbrella handles were sometimes made of whalebone.

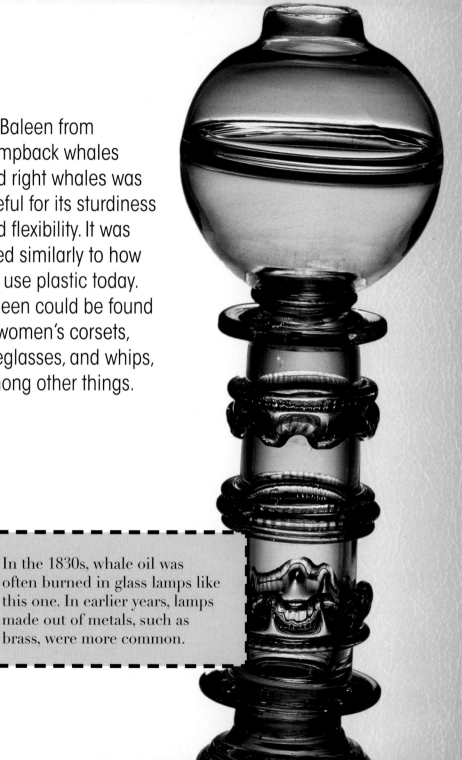

Baleen from humpback whales and right whales was useful for its sturdiness and flexibility. It was used similarly to how we use plastic today. Baleen could be found in women's corsets, eyeglasses, and whips, among other things.

In the 1830s, whale oil was often burned in glass lamps like this one. In earlier years, lamps made out of metals, such as brass, were more common.

THE COLLAPSE OF WHALING

By the end of the nineteenth century, American whalers had killed thousands of whales. The business was very dangerous. When whaling was at its peak in the nineteenth century, several ships sank every year. They took dozens of young men with them.

Most whaling ships were only about 100 feet (30 m) long. One of the biggest dangers crewmen on whaling ships faced was storms at sea.

Whales live long lives. They have babies less frequently than most other ocean animals do. This means it will take more time for their numbers to make a comeback.

Over time, the whaling industry faded out. Electricity replaced whale oil. Steel and plastic replaced baleen. Other kinds of wax replaced spermaceti for candles. Since they had been hunted for so long, whales became rarer. They were also not as valuable a **resource** as they had been. For these reasons, it became harder and harder to make money hunting whales.

WHALES TODAY

The **populations** of some whales, such as the North Atlantic right whale, are in danger. Others, such as the finback whale, are in less danger.

Some Alaskan Native American tribes are allowed to hunt a few whales each year. They give some of these to the US government for scientific study. However, commercial whale hunting is now illegal in most countries. As long as they are protected, whales will continue to roam the seas.

In many coastal American places, people go on whale-watching tours, on which they can often see humpbacks, gray whales, finbacks, and more kinds of whales.

ambergris (AM-ber-gris) A waxy substance that forms in the intestines of sperm whales.

baleen (buh-LEEN) The structure through which baleen whales strain food.

climates (KLY-muts) The kinds of weather certain places have.

colonists (KAH-luh-nists) People who move to a new place but are still ruled by the leaders of the country from which they came.

commercial (kuh-MER-shul) Having to do with business or trade.

industry (IN-dus-tree) A business in which many people work and make money producing something.

integrated (IN-tuh-gray-ted) Brought different races, genders, or social classes together to form one group.

populations (pop-yoo-LAY-shunz) Groups of animals or people living in the same place.

resource (REE-sawrs) Things that occur in nature and that can be used or sold, such as gold, coal, or wool.

scrimshaw (SKRIM-shaw) Carvings done on animal bones or teeth.

species (SPEE-sheez) One kind of living thing. All people are one species.

spermaceti (sper-muh-SEE-tee) A waxy substance found in an opening inside the heads of sperm whales.

INDEX

WEBSITES

Due to the changing nature of Internet links, PowerKids Press has developed an online list of websites related to the subject of this book. This site is updated regularly. Please use this link to access the list:

www.powerkidslinks.com/anhi/whale/